TRUSTING
GOD *In*
HARD TIMES

Lessons from the Life of Elijah

TRUSTING
GOD *In*
HARD TIMES

Lessons from the Life of Elijah

BILL CROWDER

DISCOVERY HOUSE
PUBLISHERS°

Feeding the Soul with the Word of God

P.O. Box 3566, Grand Rapids MI 49501-3566

© 2009 by RBC Ministries
Grand Rapids, Michigan
All rights reserved.

Requests for permission to quote from this book should
be directed to: Permissions Department, Discovery House
Publishers, P.O. Box 3566, Grand Rapids, MI 49501.

Scripture quotations are from
The New King James Version, © by Thomas Nelson, Inc.
All rights reserved.

Interior design by Steve Gier
Cover design by Stan Myers
Cover photo by Purestock / Getty Images

ISBN: 978-1-57293-366-8

Printed in the United States of America

09 10 11 12 / CHG_RBC / 10 9 8 7 6 5 4 3 2 1

CONTENTS

Introduction 7

Average in Greatness 11

Times of Courage 23

Times of Training 37

Times of Faith 55

Times of Conflict 75

Times of Frailty 91

A Final Word: "The Time It Is Today" 105

INTRODUCTION

IF YOU WERE TO SELECT a song as the anthem of our day, you probably wouldn't select "Happy Days Are Here Again." I do believe, however, that many would vote for "Nobody Knows The Troubles I've Seen." Those troubles can be national or local. They can be health-related or economically based. They can be personal or interpersonal.

None of those things is the core issue, however. When we enter these dark seasons of personal loss, disappointment, or even disaster, we are facing problems that can be distressing—problems that seem so overwhelming that we could drown under the weight of them.

So where do we turn?

People turn to any number of outlets—either to help them face their problems or to try to escape them. Yet in those dark seasons, what is needed most is wisdom. And for that, we would do well to turn to the pages of the Bible where examples abound of individuals who faced hard times, turned to the God who cares, and found the strength to endure.

Such a person was the Old Testament prophet Elijah. Faced with extraordinarily challenging times, Elijah turned his heart to the God of Abraham, Isaac, and Jacob. He recognized the reality that we can hear expressed in the old gospel song, "In Times Like These, We Need A Savior." And He found that his God—the one true God and not the false gods of his age—was sufficient for the times in which he lived and struggled.

We want to walk with Elijah on his faith journey. In it we will see him do right and do wrong. We will see him act wisely and act foolishly. We will see him exhibit great faith and great despair. And in it all, we will see that God never leaves him nor forsakes him.

"In Times Like These" we can learn much from Elijah the prophet. May our hearts be open to the grace and wisdom of our Lord as we learn to rest in His faithfulness.

—BILL CROWDER

9

AVERAGE IN GREATNESS

J OHN WAYNE was a movie megastar. In fact, film studios used to base their annual projections on his popularity. He was so bankable in the 1940s, 50s, and 60s that his movies consistently drew huge crowds to the theaters—many of them filled with starry-eyed boys like me. My friends and I watched the Duke's adventures breathlessly, imagining that we were riding at his side to save the day. To me, John Wayne was an American hero.

There was something about the Duke, however, that I didn't understand until I was older. Wayne was not considered a great actor by movie critics who watched him on the big screen. That was because unlike an actor such as Gregory Peck, who became lost in the role of whatever character he was playing, John Wayne was always John Wayne. Whether playing a sheriff in America's Old West, a World War II marine, or a modern-day detective, he was always himself— not the character.

This disappointing realization showed me something I didn't want to know. Although as a screen hero Wayne was larger than life, as an actor he was just average. In fact, he did not win an Oscar until he was 63 years old—after 40 years in the business. The fact that John Wayne was an average actor in the garb of greatness was a hard concept for me to understand. This reality helped me to reevaluate other assumptions in life.

A Man Like John Wayne?

This same tension hit me a few years ago when I studied the life of a great prophet of ancient

Israel. I had grown up hearing Sunday school stories about Elijah. He too captured my imagination. As an Old Testament superhero, Elijah seemed to be able to do everything short of leaping tall buildings in a single bound.

A review of the life of the prophet Elijah brings to mind some pretty strong images:

- Boldly defying a king
- Raising a boy from the dead
- Calling down fire from heaven
- Riding to heaven in a fiery chariot

And the fact that such a man appears in the pages of the Bible also helps to make him seem bigger than life. It's hard for me to imagine Elijah as just an average person, say, waiting for a bus or buying burgers at McDonald's. Yet the New Testament makes a point of letting us know that Elijah was, after all, a very ordinary person.

A Man Like Us

The New Testament says that Elijah was subject to the same emotions and moods as the rest of us. Even though his life was marked by miracles, eight words help us identify with him. The apostle James said of Elijah that he "was a man with a nature like ours" (James 5:17).

This was an important distinction for James to make for the readers of his day. Among the Old Testament characters mentioned in the New, Elijah would have ranked near the top with people such as Moses, Abraham, and David. One scholar has said this about Elijah: "No biblical figure so exercised the religious thinking of post-biblical Judaism."

New Testament Christians would have perceived Elijah to be special for several reasons. For one, they knew that he had appeared to Jesus at the transfiguration. When Jesus took His disciples to the far northern regions of Israel, he allowed Peter, James, and John to join him on "a

high mountain" (Matthew 17:1) for an amazing
visitation. As Jesus was transfigured in their
presence, Moses and Elijah appeared before them.
At that meeting, Jesus, Moses, and Elijah spoke
about Jesus' soon departure from this world.
Elijah's presence at this auspicious occasion surely
would have caused Jesus' followers to have an
elevated view of him. Yet James, who lived in that
era, nevertheless reminded his readers that Elijah
was "a man with a nature like ours."

This truth was important to the teaching
James was providing—that God has given prayer
to help us in our weakness. This statement about
Elijah reminded the early Christians that Elijah
had the same weaknesses and failures that tell the
story of our lives. And if prayer worked for him, it
could work for them.

Another reason Elijah was thought to be special
during the New Testament era was that many
people in Jesus' day thought Elijah would soon

return to minister to the people. Malachi 4:5-6 seems to indicate this eventuality. It says, "Behold, I will send you Elijah the prophet before the coming of the great and dreadful day of the Lord."

That's why many people thought John the Baptist was Elijah. Later, when Jesus asked His disciples who the crowds said He was (this happened not long before the transfiguration), they answered, "Some say John the Baptist, some Elijah, and others, Jeremiah or one of the prophets" (Matthew 16:14). Clearly, Elijah was seen by the people in the first century as a special man of God.

This prophet, whose name was known by so many in Jesus' day and who had engaged in so many amazing events back in his own time, though, was not Superman. He was, in a sense, everyman. He experienced the discouragement, fears, and doubts that mark all of us from time to time. Elijah pictures for us human frailty, spiritual dependence, and the great need for prayer in our walk with God.

A Man Of Mystery

Elijah shows up abruptly in the Old Testament record of Israel's kings, appearing on the pages of the Bible with minimal introduction—no lineage, no pedigree, and no résumé. First Kings 17:1 simply says:

"Elijah the Tishbite, of the inhabitants of Gilead . . ."

We can't even be sure what the biblical writer meant by calling him "the Tishbite." Some scholars think this is a reference to Tishbe, a city beyond Jordan, in the tribe of Gad. The word *tishbe*, however, can also be translated "pilgrim or sojourner." It could simply mean that he was homeless and wandering in Gilead before the Bible calls our attention to him.

The most we can be sure of is that Elijah is

"of the inhabitants of Gilead." Gilead was east of the Jordan River, inhabited by the tribes of Israel (Reuben, Gad, and the half-tribe of Manasseh) who, in the days of Joshua, did not enter the Land of Promise.

This lack of background provided by the biblical narrative adds to the mystique of "Elijah the Tishbite." Because he comes to us in obscurity, some writers have tried to fill in the gaps, speculating at length about his parentage, miraculous birth, and education in the school of the prophets.

What seems most apparent, however, is that the Scriptures use Elijah's obscurity to emphasize that his significance is in his God, not in himself or in his own personal accomplishments. His Hebrew name is *Eliyahu* (literally, Yah is El), signifying that Jehovah is God. As his story unfolds, we see the significance of his name—Elijah was sent to demonstrate to Israel that Yah (Jehovah), not Baal, is the one true God.

A Man For Extraordinary Times

American writer and philosopher Ralph Waldo Emerson said of the era in which he was writing: "This time, like all times, is a very good one, if we but know what to do with it." Emerson, who wrote those words in the mid 1800s, reminds us that our response to the conditions of our lives is more important than the nature of our circumstances.

Elijah is an ancient showcase for such wisdom. There are only a few periods in the Bible when we see a wave of "sign miracles." In most periods of history, the servants of God do not go around healing the sick, raising the dead, and calling down fire from heaven.

Yet Elijah and his protégé Elisha lived in one of those exceptional times. The miracles that distinguished their public lives paralleled the supernatural display of power that marked two other periods of history. Much earlier, during Israel's supernatural exodus, the miracles of

Moses had shown that God was delivering Israel from slavery in Egypt. Many years later, the miracles of Christ and His apostles would make it clear that the same God was delivering people of all nations and all times from the spiritual penalty and bondage of sin.

So what was happening in the days of Elijah that required such a supernatural display?

The northern kingdom of Israel had begun to slide into the darkness of idolatry. A succession of ungodly kings had led the kingdom into this decline. One after the other was described in Scripture as doing "evil in the sight of the Lord" (1 Kings 15:26). From Jeroboam to Nadab to Baasha—seven kings in all continued to turn their backs on God and rule in ways that saddened Him.

It all culminated in the reign of Ahab, about whom Scripture says, he "did evil in the sight of the Lord, more than all who were before him" (1 Kings 16:30). Among the evil things

Ahab did was to marry Jezebel, an outsider from Phoenicia, and to set up Baal worship throughout the kingdom.

In fact, spiritual conditions had deteriorated so much that Elijah mistakenly thought he was the only person who still believed in the God of Israel (1 Kings 19:10). In one of the darkest times of Israel's history, God used Elijah to show Himself as Lord of lords and God of gods. While the kings mistakenly felt that they were the ones with authority and the ability to shape the lives of their subjects, God interrupted their reigns to remind them that He was in control. At this extraordinary time in the history of the Jewish people, the person God used to accomplish that intervention was an ordinary man from Gilead—Elijah.

TIMES OF COURAGE

OUR INITIAL GLIMPSE at Elijah shows him to be a man of courage—courage that comes to those who live in God's presence. Elijah, the Tishbite, who lived among the inhabitants of Gilead, stood boldly before the king and declared to Ahab, "As the Lord God of Israel lives, before whom I stand, there shall not be dew nor rain these years, except at my word" (1 Kings 17:1).

With these few words, Elijah stepped into the pages of the Bible and right into the middle of a hornet's nest.

Israel's economy was based on agriculture. Now, in response to Elijah's prayer, God was about to withhold the seasonal rains from a people who needed them to grow their crops. Why? This was a wake-up call to His people. It was a moment of corrective judgment.

As noted above, Israel had fallen into Baal worship under the direction of Ahab. He built a temple to Baal in Samaria, the capital of the northern kingdom, and he had "set up an Asherah pole" (1 Kings 16:33), an object that was associated with pagan worship.

Ahab bowed before false gods who could do nothing either way about rain or drought. Elijah's pronouncement of an upcoming drought set up a direct contrast between his God and the one Ahab chose. Baal was the fertility god, and he was also referred to as the "rainmaker god." Not so, Elijah's words suggest. Jehovah is in charge of the water that falls from the sky, he seems to be saying, and He's going to prove it.

The removal of rain in an already dry climate

would be a crippling blow to the agricultural-based community—but God was about to demonstrate to the people that it was far more important to trust Him than to have the refreshing and life-giving rains.

As the corrective hand of God was about to fall upon His people, Elijah—a nobody from nowhere—stepped boldly into the palace of King Ahab to speak truth in the halls of power.

25

Ahab's Sin

When the northern kingdom of Israel and the southern kingdom of Judah separated after the time of Solomon's rule, Jeroboam became king in the north and Rehoboam took charge in the south. Both kings set in motion a series of poor decisions that would have far-reaching implications for both kingdoms: Jeroboam and Rehoboam both set up idol worship.

In Israel, this violation of the first commandment

of the law Moses had received on the mountain and brought down to the people became a pattern that would lead all the way to Ahab. Jeroboam started the spiral downward by creating two golden calves for the people to worship (1 Kings 12:28). Fearful that his subjects would desire to go to the temple in Jerusalem (which was in the southern kingdom) to worship—and would subsequently transfer their allegiance to Judah's king Rehoboam, Jeroboam offered the people his two golden idols. "He said to the people, 'It is too much for you to go up to Jerusalem. Here are your gods, O Israel, who brought you up from the land of Egypt' " (v. 28).

With this action, Jeroboam started Israel down that long road of evil and idol worship mentioned earlier. Most of those kings angered God "with their idols" (1 Kings 16:13, 26).

Then along came Ahab. When it came to a life committed to evil, he out-did all of them.

"Now Ahab the son of Omri did evil in the sight of the Lord, more than all who were before him" (1 Kings 16:30). He copied and even multiplied the sinful practices of the first king, Jeroboam, 60 years earlier. Ahab introduced Baal worship to the people of Israel—a form of idol-keeping that came along with Jezebel from her homelands of Tyre and Sidon (v.31).

In fact, Ahab did not simply favor Baal worship; he raised it to the same level of importance as worship of God. Review 1 Kings 16:32, which explains that Ahab constructed a temple in Samaria and reveals that in that temple was an altar to Baal. The parallels between Solomon's temple in Jerusalem and Baal's temple in Samaria are hard to miss. Clearly, Ahab put another god before the one true God.

This 60-year stretch of evil kings was not the first time God's people would forget the One who delivered them from Egypt, provided for them in the wilderness, and led them into this Promised Land. From the days of Sinai and the golden calf to the time of Ezekiel and the idol-infested Holy of Holies, God's chosen people were often seduced by the gods of the land.

As we look back at the people of Israel and their error, we may think this kind of thing cannot happen in the twenty-first century. We may consider ourselves too enlightened and too sophisticated to engage in something so primitive as idol worship. Yet, idolatry is nothing more than putting something else—anything else—in the place of God. In his book *Unwavering Tenacity: Insights into the Life of Elijah,* Bible teacher Gene Getz suggests that we do this today on several levels. He says some of us may have these gods:

• Humanistic Gods. This includes a wide array of people such as sports stars, musicians, and leaders.

- Materialistic Gods. "You cannot serve both God and Money" (Matthew 6:24 NIV), or the things that money buys.
- Sensual Gods. "For this you know, that no fornicator, unclean person, nor covetous man, who is an idolater, has any inheritance in the kingdom of Christ and God" (Ephesians 5:5).
- Relational Gods. Even something as wonderful as healthy relationships can become idols. Jesus warned, "He who loves father or mother more than Me is not worthy of Me. And he who loves son or daughter more than Me is not worthy of Me" (Matthew 10:37).

Through Elijah, God confronted Ahab about what Paul warns us against in Romans 1:25—worshiping the creature instead of the Creator. The apostle's words clearly define the sin of the king of Israel: "They exchanged the truth of God for a lie, and worshiped and served created things rather than the Creator."

God's Response

When Elijah stood before Ahab, he told the king: "There shall not be dew nor rain these years, except at my word" (1 Kings 17:1).

Bible teacher John Whitcomb wrote about the mystery and the intrigue of Elijah's words. "Like a meteor suddenly flashing across the darkened sky, Elijah appears on the scene without genealogy, without historical background, and without warning. One thunderous judgment from heaven through his lips, and he disappeared without a trace!" (*Solomon To The Exile*, p.50).

We don't see Ahab's immediate response. We don't find out if Elijah was run out of the palace by the guards. According to the biblical record (1 Kings 17), he simply spoke his God-sent message and was gone. He left Ahab's presence and headed for his next appointed location, which we see revealed to him in verses 2 and 3 of chapter 17.

Elijah's message to Ahab had a strong precedent. Years before, Moses had warned that national apostasy would cause the rains to cease (Deuteronomy 11:16-17). He told the people, "Take heed to yourselves, lest your heart be deceived, and you turn aside and serve other gods and worship them, lest the Lord's anger be aroused against you, and He shut up the heavens so that there be no rain, and the land yield no produce, and you perish quickly from the good land which the Lord is giving you" (vv.16-17).

God was reminding Moses and the people of his day that He was in charge of the seasonal rains that allowed the people to grow their crops and live. His ability to control this aspect of their lives would have had at least two messages to them. First, it would remind them that it was the one true God who was in charge—not Baal, the god of many of the Canaanites. Second, it would remind the people that if God was actively involved in their lives, He expected obedience from them.

Despite the repeated warnings, though, Israel had been unfaithful to her God. So, as Ahab had been warned, God's blessings on the land would be suspended. Under Ahab's watch, the land would experience more than three years of drought.

Elijah's Prayer

James 5:17-18 tells us that prayer was the means God used to signal and release these events of judgment on the land of Israel. It's amazing that a seeming nobody like Elijah could have the kind of spiritual boldness and courage that would allow him to be such a successful prayer warrior. Remember that James tells us he "was a man with a nature like ours."

This was an important distinction to make in the New Testament era. Elijah was undoubtedly one of the most hallowed historical characters among the people of James' day. When James told his readers that they and Elijah were of the same nature—that Elijah was "a man just like us" as one translation puts it—he was emphasizing that this great Old Testament man was no different from each of them. James' readers then and believers today are being encouraged that they could have a prayer life just as effective as did the one enjoyed by this great figure in biblical history.

While no mention is made of Elijah's prayer in 1 Kings, we learn from what James tells us that Elijah met three prayer criteria when he offered up his petition to God during hard times. James was saying that we should emulate these measures as we pray.

First, James alluded to the fact that Elijah was "a righteous man" (v. 16). He was a person just like us, but he was clearly godly. To be righteous

33

does not mean that Elijah was perfect; it means that when Elijah prayed, he had confessed his sin and had been forgiven. He was in good standing with God, the author of righteousness.

Second, James tells us that Elijah prayed "earnestly" for the rain to be withheld. And it was! "He prayed earnestly that it would not rain; and it did not rain on the land for three years and six months" (v. 17). The essence of verses 16 and 17 tell us of both the power of prayer and the usefulness of prayer. Prayer is powerful—and intense praying is what Elijah did. And it worked!

Third, Elijah also prayed specifically. He prayed that there would be no dew or rain—no moistening at all. The answer to his prayer was in the dry details of the drought that followed.

For 3 ½ years, God used the prayers of a man like us to confront some people who had drifted away from His love.

Applying It

Elijah understood the power of prayer, and he practiced it—giving us some key questions to consider:

• Do we think that our effectiveness for God is dependent on our talents or position? Or are we dependent on God Himself?

• Do we see the true God as the one and only object of our worship? Or are our hearts and minds clouded by other gods?

• Do we live in the reality of the resource of prayer, through which God can do amazing things according to His will?

35

TIMES
OF TRAINING

SEVERAL YEARS AGO, sports-shoe maker Nike ran a series of ads themed, "What are you getting ready for?" One showed an NFL football player throwing himself down a steep, rocky hill. Another had a soccer player doing everything in life with his feet. The point? What we do today is getting us ready for something that we will be involved in later.

What are you getting ready for? Whatever it is, training will be needed:

• Hours at the piano learning scales and practicing sonatas;

• Days in the hot August sun enduring two-a-day football practices;

• Years in a laboratory preparing for a career in medical research.

It seems that for much of life there are seasons of preparation. And the more intense something is, the more intense the training will be. This was true for Elijah as well. God had a plan to build more depth of trust and character into his servant. Bible teacher J. Vernon McGee wrote:

> You get the impression that Elijah was a rugged individual, and he was. But there's something else that should be said here about him—God had to train this man. God has always had a method of training the men He uses by taking them to the desert . . . . This is God's method for training His men. Now He is going to take out this man Elijah and teach him several things he needs to learn (*Thru The Bible*, Vol II, p.283).

God's Direction

Immediately after we read of Elijah's pronouncement to Ahab, we are informed anew about Elijah's willingness to obey God. By a direct message, Elijah is ordered to take himself out of the normal realm of life and go to the wilderness.

"Then the word of the Lord came to him, saying, 'Get away from here and turn eastward, and hide by the Brook Cherith, which flows into the Jordan. And it will be that you shall drink from the brook, and I have commanded the ravens to feed you there' " (1 Kings 17:2-4).

Gilead was east of the Jordan River, so God was sending Elijah back home to a brook that was no more than a wadi—a seasonal stream that carries water only during the winter rains. Wadi Cherith seems like an unusual place for God to provide food and water during a three-year drought. Perhaps there was a cave or a shelter there. We don't know. What we do know, however, is that Wadi Cherith

39

is in the teeth of the wilderness—a hard place to live and a hard place to learn.

We also know that there was an element of danger involved. If someone tells you to go to a certain location to meet someone or to take a break from the routine of life, that's one thing. But if you are told to "get away" from here and "hide" as the passage above does, that's far different. There is certainly an element of threat involved. We know from reading a later passage (1 Kings 18:4) that God's prophets were not safe in the land controlled by Ahab and his wife Jezebel.

Therefore, as soon as Elijah made his pronouncement to Ahab, God spoke to him and gave him a getaway route. Despite Elijah's evident courage, one can imagine the pressure that was on him as he took off for the wilderness—never knowing if Ahab's men might be hunting him down.

Elijah would have to travel over 15-20 miles on foot through barren land to arrive at a less-than-hospitable place. But this is where God sent him. Elijah had much to learn, and the days of solitude would furnish much-needed moments of reflection and learning.

Elijah's Response

God spoke, and Elijah responded. From the palace to the wilderness he went without delay. "So he went and did according to the word of the Lord, for he went and stayed by the Brook Cherith, which flows into the Jordan" (1 Kings 17:5).

Notice that God made promises to Elijah that were directly linked to his response: He obeyed God's Word, believed God's promise, and went to the Wadi Cherith. As a result, God would make good on His promise to meet his physical needs. Undoubtedly, faith is always a critical issue in a believer's relationship with God, and Elijah responded with trust and obedience.

Elijah made the long trek to a lonely place and

settled in there. It must have been an interesting first day at Cherith. Did he watch the skies, wondering if ravens would really show up? This was a new experience for Elijah. The imagination of German biographer F. W. Krummacher gives us a possible look at Elijah in his new environs:

> Come, let us pay a visit to this man of God in his new dwelling place. A dreary wild, near the banks of the Jordan, is the scene now opened before us. Dead silence reigns around, interrupted perhaps by the cry of the solitary bittern, while amongst the heath and juniper bushes broods the ostrich—no hunter disturbing its repose. No pathway opens to the view—not a human footstep is seen—all is wilderness and solitude . . . . There sits the man of God. Here is his appointed dwelling: the blue sky his roof, the bare rocks his walls, the stone his seat,

the shady wood his bed-chamber, the grass
his couch; his company, the purling brook,
and the hoarse ravens aloft among the trees
(*Elijah the Tishbite*, pp. 34-35).

Imagine the isolation he felt. Alone in the
desert, Elijah would learn of his God in this hard
place. Because he had obeyed, he had assurance
of God's care and provision.

43

God's Provision

Sometimes when God directs His people to
go, he simply gives them map directions. For
instance, when Abraham was told to leave Haran
and head for a land about which God said, "I will
show you" (Genesis 12:1), no food provisions were
given. Just go. But in this case, God not only told
Elijah where He wanted him to go, He also told
him how He was going to feed him during his
time there (1 Kings 17:4).

And it happened just as God said it would. "The ravens brought him bread and meat in the morning, and bread and meat in the evening; and he drank from the brook" (v. 6)

There at Wadi Cherith, God's promised provision nourished Elijah. Notice how God provided:

• Ravens, voracious birds of prey, would never naturally relinquish their food. Perhaps God used these particular birds to impress upon Elijah the real source of his food so he would trust God for His provision instead of the birds themselves.

• Bread and meat twice a day (compared to the manna and quail in the wilderness).

• Water from Cherith.

Examined separately, each of these elements of God's provision can help us understand Elijah even better.

Ravens: Imagine Elijah's surprise when God announced to him that ravens would be his food service providers. Ravens! Surely Elijah knew about Leviticus 11:13-19. In those verses, which are part of a chapter that explains all of the unclean foods that Jewish people were to avoid, we read, "These are the birds you are to detest and not eat because they are detestable: the eagle, the vulture, the black vulture, the red kite, any kind of black kite, any kind of raven" (vv.13-14).

Ravens are scavengers. They eat carrion. They are unclean—both in reality and in matters of faith.

Bread and meat twice a day. We are not told where the ravens were able to obtain bread or what condition the meat was in when the ravens brought it to Elijah, but we know this for sure. Elijah had to exercise extreme faith as he awaited his food. There were no reserves. No snacks. No assurance, other than God's promise that he would have enough food to sustain him each day.

Water from the wadi. There is a certain irony to the combination of events that God called on

Elijah to be involved in. First, God asked him to declare a long-term drought in the land. Then, He sent him to live where he would be totally dependent on rain for his sustenance to continue. The Brook Cherith depended on rains to fill its banks and send water down to the Jordan. Eventually, we assume, the drought would dry up the wadi, leaving Elijah without resources.

God provided in unique ways for Elijah—ways that at first look would appear to be difficult and worrisome for most. But Elijah, a man of faith and action, did not hesitate to trust God's provision.

God always uses the proper means to accomplish His purposes and training in the lives of His children. This is true whether those means are natural (Wadi Cherith) or supernatural (raven-delivered sandwiches). He remains Jehovah-Jireh, "the Lord will provide."

God's faithfully kept promises and His unusual provisions are key elements of Elijah's preparation.

Elijah's Training

You have to wonder what went through Elijah's mind as he waited each day by the Brook Cherith. Between feedings by the big birds, did he spend his time thinking about his adventure before Ahab? Did he spend a lot of time praying? Did he wonder how things were going back home in Gilead?

For some reason, this was the training ground that God had planned for Elijah. Whether he was praying, pining, remembering, or simply trying to survive, he was learning more and more each day about trusting God.

You also have to wonder how Elijah received the news from God about his next move. For a man living alone in the wilderness, it must have presented some encouragement to know that his next move would include people.

Here's the account of how God told Elijah what he would do next: "And it happened after a while that the brook dried up, because there had been no rain in the land. Then the word of the Lord came to him, saying, 'Arise, go to Zarephath, which belongs to Sidon, and dwell there. See, I have commanded a widow there to provide for you.' So he arose and went to Zarephath" (1 Kings 17:7-10).

Bible teachers believe that Elijah was in the wilderness for more than a year. And even though food arrived daily, his anxiety level must have been rising. For as the drought continued, the river became a stream, then a creek, then a mere trickle.

This was part of God's training of Elijah. Imagine what must have been happening to the prophet's faith as the water level in the brook dipped lower and lower. God could have brought water from the rocks, as He had for Israel in the wilderness, but He didn't. The water was running out.

Remember, Elijah was "a man like us." How might he have responded:

- Wanting to panic? He knew where to get

water. He knew where the Jordan and other rivers were. What would stop him from leaving the wilderness behind to find what he needed?

• Wanting to give up and die? (as he later desired).

• Wanting to reverse God's judgment because it was affecting him personally?

This is all part of the training process. Elijah needed to know that he could trust God for more than water, even in the desert, and even when the brook dried up. He needed to learn that:

God knew all along that the brook would dry up. It was inevitable. The wadi was dependent on the heavy rains of late autumn and early winter. And when those rains did not arrive, the brook disappeared.

God's care was not hampered when the brook dried up. It would be easy for Elijah to assume that he had been forgotten by God. But he had to learn that he was dependent on God, not on the brook.

God was still in control, even when the brook dried up. In fact, God was so thoroughly in control that

49

He totally disrupted the comfort zone Elijah had become used to. Why? To stretch him in new ways.

When our comfort zone is shattered, it doesn't mean that God has lost control. But it may mean that we've stopped hearing the voice of God because we've grown too comfortable.

Even as the water receded, Elijah stayed at the brook until he was instructed to go elsewhere: "Arise, go" (v.9). The lessons of trusting and obedience were being imprinted on his heart.

So God sent him from the wadi on a journey to Zarephath.

What do we know about Elijah's next destination?

• It was 80-90 miles northwest of Cherith, on the Mediterranean seacoast in Gentile, not Jewish, land.

• It was in the heart of a land dominated by Baal worship.

• It was the homeland of Queen Jezebel, priestess of Baal, the god that Elijah had challenged. And, of course, Jezebel was the wife of the king whom Elijah had challenged.

It appears that Elijah was moving from the frying pan directly into the fire. He was a devoted God-worshiper heading into a land that worshiped idols. He was a Jew moving into the middle of the Gentiles. And he was the bearer of bad news going into the territory of the spouse to whom he bore that news. However, none of those considerations rose to the level of being included in the scriptural account. Instead, Elijah's journey to Zarephath had drama of a far different kind.

When God told Elijah to take this journey, what did He tell the prophet he would find there?

A widow to care for him. That's not very promising. Widows were normally the poorest of the poor. In this economy they lived on the fringes of society with no one to take care of them. They were vulnerable and unprotected. In a time of famine, they would be the first to run out of food, not the last.

This is not the most encouraging news a man could receive.

Elijah was leaving behind a dried-up brook and a bunch of bread-snatching, meat-providing ravens, and he was exchanging those harsh realities for the prospect of being cared for by a down-and-out widow. This didn't appear to be an upgrade for the prophet on the run.

Why did God command Elijah in this way? Why did he command Elijah to go into hostile territory so he could find someone who would have no means for taking care of him? Because God is training His servant to walk by faith, not by sight—and nobody said it would be easy.

Welcome to Elijah's world, as he personally experiences the power (and price tag) of spiritual training. Author W. J. Petersen writes:

> Sometimes we don't understand God's
> dealings. We don't know why we were sent to

Cherith in the first place; we don't appreciate the fact that God uses dirty ravens to feed us; and we certainly don't understand why the brook has to dry up. The fact that we don't understand is simply a sign that God's educational process isn't complete yet. He is still teaching us and we're still learning (*Meet Me On The Mountain*, p.44).

Applying It

What lessons can we learn from the "Wadi Cherith Training Center For Spiritual Service"?

• Sometimes God's children suffer along with unbelievers.

• Sometimes when we think we are ready for Mount Carmel, God sends us to Cherith because we are not as ready as we think.

• Sometimes God's hiding place isn't an easy place.

TIMES
OF FAITH

SOMEONE HAS DEFINED "faith" with the acrostic, "Forsaking All I Trust Him." This certainly describes what Elijah did in the stories recorded about him in 1 Kings 17. He forsook all to trust God. After he confronted King Ahab and ridiculed his idol Baal, he escaped into the wilderness under God's direction. For at least a year, he had to trust God to provide for him in a desolate place and in a miraculous way.

Elijah's first lesson in trust, then, was that God could provide for him. But God was not done teaching. Elijah's next lesson was to learn that God could provide for others as well. Life wasn't simply about Elijah—he had to see the needs of others and respond with a God-directed concern for them. Elijah would learn that lesson in Zarephath.

A Woman's Testing

For the third time in the short record we have of Elijah's life until now, he listens to and heeds God's call for him to exercise his faith. Although we don't have the background story that describes how Elijah ended up in the presence of Ahab to warn him about the upcoming drought, we can imagine that the "word of the Lord" about this "came to Elijah" just as it would do later when God told him to go to the Brook Cherith and when He told the prophet to go to Zarephath. We can assume that God gave Elijah specific instructions about his proclamation to the king.

Each time, Elijah had to set aside his own feelings—perhaps his fear, for instance—to do God's bidding. And each time, he forsook all—he set aside all of his hesitations to do what God asked him to do. We don't know anything about Elijah's family, for instance, but we can assume that when he left Gilead to confront Ahab, he had to set aside his family to make that trip.

Now he is being called to leave behind the ravens, the dried-up brook, and his wilderness hideout to travel to Zarephath for an encounter with a widow. "So he arose and went to Zarephath. And when he came to the gate of the city, indeed a widow was there gathering sticks" (1 Kings 17:10).

Clearly, God directed Elijah to know exactly which woman he wanted the prophet to notice and meet after arriving at Zarephath. It had been a long walk from the parched wadi at Cherith, and Elijah was thirsty. So his first words to the widow consisted of a request: "Please bring me a little water in a cup, that I may drink" (v.10).

Perhaps this was Elijah's initial test of God's promise. He had been told, "I have commanded a widow there to provide for you" (v. 9). So he asked for water—but not just water. As the widow walked away to get the requested refreshment, Elijah called out after her. "Please bring me a morsel of bread in your hand" (v. 11).

The request for bread was a little too much for the widow to fulfill, as we will see, but Elijah's trust in God was rewarded. He had sent the prophet across Israel to Zarephath and right into the home of a woman who believed in the one true God. Upon hearing Elijah's initial request for her, the first recorded words she said to him were, "As the Lord your God lives" (v.12).

Imagine the music those words were to Elijah's ears. After confronting the idol-worshiping king and then after living by himself in the wilderness, just think of how delightful it was to discover that the appointed widow was a kindred spirit! Surely this was another indicator to Elijah that trusting God's instructions was the right thing to do.

For the next 2 years, Elijah would be supported by this woman. And though he would soon discover how poor she was, he must have found great comfort in the fact that now there were two people trusting God for their provision—not just one.

Immediately their trust in God was put to the test.

When Elijah asked her for a "morsel of bread," her response was anything but encouraging. "I do not have bread," she explained. "Only a handful of flour in a bin, and a little oil in a jar" (v.12).

And then she dropped a huge surprise on this visitor.

"I am gathering a couple of sticks that I may go in and prepare it for myself and my son, that we may eat it, and die" (v.12).

There were indeed *three* people to feed here—and there simply was not enough food.

This is when the trust element took on a new dimension for the widow. Elijah asked her to feed him first. But when he did, he also made her an outrageous promise.

In effect, he said to her, "If you feed me first, then make some food for yourself and you son, you will not run out of food."

"The bin of flour shall not be used up, nor shall the jar of oil run dry, until the day the Lord sends rain on the earth," Elijah told her (v.14).

What a dilemma for the widow/mother!

Think about it. Elijah requested a meal for himself and promised her some provisions (v.14), but he didn't give her any evidence that he could keep his promise. She had two options:

• Eat the last of her food, believing that death was imminent.

• Give Elijah her last food and trust his promise that God would provide.

She had just met this newcomer to town. She knew nothing about him but that he said he could somehow make sure she didn't run out of oil for new food. She had no proof that God would keep Elijah's promises. Would you give up your last meal for a stranger with no known history?

Remember:

"Faith is the substance of things hoped for, the evidence of things not seen" (Hebrews 11:1).

The woman responded in faith to what she hoped for, yet could not see.

"She went away and did according to the word of Elijah" (v.15). He asked her to feed him first, and when she obeyed, the God of provision blessed her. As a result, the widow, her son, and Elijah "ate for many days" (v.15).

God's constant supply of flour and oil for this woman was a miracle. It pictures Jesus' promise in Matthew 6:33, "Seek first the kingdom of God and His righteousness, and all these things shall be added to you." She put God's purposes first, and God graciously provided.

The widow of Zarephath was tested by an out-of-town prophet who showed up one day with some outlandish requests, and she passed the exam victoriously.

A Family's Crisis

Because of God's provision of food for the family, the son did not starve to death—which must have given confidence to his mother. Unfortunately, a new crisis came along to threaten the widow's son. He became very sick. In fact, he was so sick that he stopped breathing. "Now it happened after these things that the son of the woman who owned the house became sick," the record tells us. "And his sickness was so serious that there was no breath left in him" (v.17).

This was a family crisis that made the earlier incident seem small by comparison.

The miracle of the never-ending foodstuffs lost its glamour when the widow's son became ill. We are not told at this time that he died—only that he had no breath.

There is no greater crisis for a mother than to see her child in danger. This poor widow's only son was her one joy in the midst of poverty and on-the-edge living—and now she seems to have lost him to an invisible enemy that she couldn't fight.

On the face of it, we would say, "That's not fair. She did everything right. She trusted, obeyed, and had a servant's heart. What more could she do?"

63

One lesson of the widow's apparent tragedy is this: If we think that trusting and obeying God exempts us from problems, we're mistaken. God is not a genie in a bottle who does whatever we want at our bidding and at our convenience. God is totally good and all-powerful, but we don't control Him. He doesn't give us a blank check to spend as we see fit.

Both Elijah and the widow had to learn that

God is in control—and so must we. We must recognize and trust the purposes of God, even in the painful crises of life.

A Mother's Pain

It is natural for those who are facing the tragedy of an unexpected death to seek out answers to the big "Why?" question. Our natural inclination is to attribute meaning to such inexplicable events, and often that leads us to try to figure out who is to blame for the tragedy.

For reasons we cannot fully understand, the widow of Zarephath turned her questioning finger at Elijah—the out-of-town guest who had invited himself into her house. Perhaps she felt that Elijah, who seemed to have a connection with God, had attracted God's attention to her. And maybe, she could have reasoned, since God was paying close attention to her household because of Elijah, He saw sin in her life and that meant punishment for her. And that punishment, she may have reasoned, was being meted out through the death of her son.

We cannot know for sure why she came to the conclusion that Elijah was the fall guy in this drama, but we know from the text that she was blaming him. She said to Elijah, "What have I to do with you, O man of God? Have you come to me to bring my sin to remembrance, and to kill my son?" (v.18).

Look at the inner battle raging in her heart:

Anger. "What have I to do with you, O man of God?" Sadly, in times of pain, we often lash out at those closest to us—even those who have done much for us. It's as if she said, "I wish you had never come." Elijah's presence in her household somehow sparked in her a feeling of anger. Her mention of his being a "man of God" would indicate that she felt that God was paying special attention to him and his situation in her household.

Guilt. "Have you come to me to bring my sin

to remembrance?" This came from her suspicion that the proximity of a prophet enabled God to see her sins more clearly. How many times does guilt play into a tragedy that we face? We are left thinking: I should have done something different so this wouldn't have happened.

Blame. "And to kill my son?" We are not told specifically why she thought God was judging her, but she was sure that her son's apparent death was payment for her sin. Perhaps this widow, who did believe in God, also had some pagan beliefs mixed up in her thought system—which would explain her thinking that the gods (or God) were in some way plotting against her.

A Prophet's Compassion

What would we do, given this situation? There on the couch lies a non-breathing child—the only hope of the future and happiness for a woman who has already lost the companionship and love of her husband. She lashes out at an uninvited visitor who had earlier had the audacity to ask her for her last morsel of food. Now she accuses him of causing the apparent death of her beloved offspring. It is a scene of extreme sadness and despair.

How would we respond if we had been accused of causing this apparent tragedy?

Would we react verbally to the mother's claims, denying our involvement in her son's demise?

Or would we do what Elijah, the ordinary prophet, did.

Without a retort to the widow's words of anger, guilt, and blame, he simply said to her, "Give me your son" (v. 19). Then he scooped the boy into his arms, rushed him outside the house to the stairs that led to Elijah's room on the roof, and he placed the boy on his own bed.

Notice how tenderly and how confidently Elijah responded to the heartache of this woman.

He took the boy "out of her arms" and hurried to his own room where he could be alone with the boy and with God.

Soon enough he will have a chance to speak again to the widow, but for now Elijah's words are reserved for and directed to his heavenly Father.

Elijah's Prayer. Look more closely at Elijah's prayer to God. Calling out to the God who had sent him to Zarephath, Elijah cried, "O Lord my God, have you also brought tragedy on the widow with whom I lodge, by killing her son?" (v. 20). Following the accusatory pattern of the widow, Elijah seems to be shifting the blame for this terrible turn of events to God. The mother blamed Elijah; now Elijah directs accusations at God Himself. It is a bold prayer, perhaps even a presumptuous prayer.

This part of the prayer was followed by an unusual but apparently important action by Elijah. He stretched himself out on the non-breathing child three times before continuing his prayer. We don't know exactly why he took this action, but we do know that two other times in Scripture men of God did this while seeking God's power to bring life back into a child. In 2 Kings 4:34, Elisha twice stretched out over a child who had died, prayed for the child, and saw him revived. And in Acts 20, a youngster by the name of Eutychus fell out of a window and died. Paul rushed to his aid, "threw himself on the young man, and put his arms around him" (v. 10). Life returned to Eutychus immediately.

As Elijah stretched himself out on the child, he cried out to the Lord and said, "O Lord my God, I pray, let this child's soul come back to him" (vv.20-21).

This confident prayer of Elijah reminds us of the lesson of James 5—the lesson illustrated by another prayer of the prophet: A prayer for rain. That was an earnest prayer, as was this one. It was presented by "a righteous man," as was this one. And it was "powerful and effective," as was this one. Once more, Elijah implored God for help when he was unable to give hope to those who needed it.

In Elijah's dual prayers in verses 20 and 21 he displayed a mix of emotions.

Elijah's Confusion. In the first prayer, it is clear that Elijah was puzzled, openly questioning God about His purposes. Remember, Elijah was a man like us (James 5:17), and we too are often confused by life. How often do we see situations around us that do not make sense in our finite understanding? So we wonder, "What is God up to now?" The good news is that God doesn't reject our honest questions. It's our arrogant demands that He refuses.

Even in the midst of Elijah's confusion, we see in his second prayer (v.21) the evidence that he is learning to grasp the greatness of God. How? Consider this amazing fact: Elijah was asking God for something that had never before happened in human history. There is no recorded instance from Genesis to 1 Kings 17 of God ever raising someone from the dead. Elijah was asking for something new in human experience. So just the fact that it occurred to him to ask God for such a miracle is amazing. Why? Because he believed in a God who could do the impossible.

God's Answer. Imagine the joy that must have gripped Elijah's heart at what happened next! "Then the Lord heard the voice of Elijah; and the soul of the child came back to him, and he revived" (v.22). The effectual, fervent prayer of Elijah reached God's ears, and He restored breath into the boy's mouth and lungs. An ordinary man prayed and an extraordinary miracle happened!

"And Elijah took the child and brought him down from the upper room into the house, and gave him to his mother. And Elijah said, 'See, your son lives!' " (v.23).

The hopes of the widow and Elijah were

rewarded. Life returned to the boy. Imagine the woman's joy as she saw her son—breathing again!

Her response is the response of the redeemed—the response of all who see God for who He is in greatness, majesty, and power. Her words that followed the miraculous return of her son to health are the words of all who have seen God's work in their lives: "Now by this I know that you are a man of God, and that the word of the Lord in your mouth is the truth" (v. 24). To see God's activities, either through reading about them in the Bible or through seeing them carried out in our lives is to see truth in action.

For the widow and for Elijah, God's purpose was now evident. Her sin was not the issue. God's purpose was to stretch the trust that both she and Elijah had in God.

Applying It

It's true that we can't control what happens to

us, but we can control how we respond to what happens to us.

- In times of crisis, are we learning to run to God's presence and care?
- In times of crisis, are we learning to face anything that might be weakening our trust in God?
- In times of crisis, are we learning to trust in God's will, not only for the future but also in the present?
- In times of crisis, are we learning to look to the power of the God of resurrection?

73

TIMES
OF CONFLICT

PILATE ASKED JESUS, "What is truth?" (John 18:38). People are still asking that question today. At the heart of so much of the cultural and religious confusion that surrounds society in the twenty-first century is the fact that so many people do not think absolute truth exists.

The issue was the same in Elijah's day—the people had rejected the God of truth for the lies of the gods of the land. Truth had been lost in a culture of idolatry.

In the time that had elapsed after the prophet left Zarephath, the stage had been set for the ultimate showdown. The time had come for the lies of the false gods to be exposed to God's truth—on the idolatrous high place of Mount Carmel. On Carmel, the priests of Baal and Asherah—850 in number (1 Kings 18:19)—stood in opposition to the God of Israel and His lone representative, Elijah.

The Issue is Clarified

Elijah had made his way east from Zarephath and arrived in the presence of Ahab for a second meeting with the king. He did this in response to God's command to him during his third year in Zarephath. "Go, present yourself to Ahab," the Lord told Elijah, "and I will send rain on the earth" (1 Kings 18:1).

When Elijah arrived at Ahab's, the king said to him, "Is that you, O troubler of Israel?" (v. 17).

The prophet responded by telling Ahab to order a meeting on Mount Carmel.

"So Ahab sent for all the children of Israel, and he gathered the prophets together on Mount

Carmel. And Elijah came to all the people, and said, 'How long will you falter between two opinions? If the Lord is God, follow Him; but if Baal, follow him.' But the people answered him not a word" (vv. 20-21).

Elijah opened with a direct question: "How long will you falter between two opinions?" (v.21). On behalf of the God of Israel, he confronted the people for their double-mindedness and told them they had to choose. The people Elijah addressed were trying to live in two worlds: They were worshiping Baal while also professing a belief in Yahweh. It was time to stop trying to have it both ways, Elijah was saying. "If the Lord is God, follow Him; but if Baal, follow him," he challenged them.

How appropriate that challenge is to our world today! We can truly serve and worship only one God with our whole heart, yet how many are the times we "go limping between two different opinions" as the English Standard Version translates Elijah's challenge? Placing trust in the one true God through Jesus is the basis for our eternity. Where will we place our trust?

Notice the crowd's silence to Elijah's challenge: "The people answered him not a word." They didn't know how to respond. It's dangerous to waffle on eternal issues, so Elijah demanded that they decide whom they were going to follow. And he was about to make it easy for them to see why they should follow God.

The Conditions are Set

Elijah seemed to be calling all the shots in this confrontation. First, he told Ahab to gather "all Israel" (v.19), and then he explained where they should go. Elijah was setting up the confrontation by his own ground rules. However, he was not setting them up to his advantage, as the text shows.

"Then Elijah said to the people, 'I alone am

left a prophet of the Lord; but Baal's prophets are four hundred and fifty men. Therefore let them give us two bulls; and let them choose one bull for themselves, cut it in pieces, and lay it on the wood, but put no fire under it; and I will prepare the other bull, and lay it on the wood, but put no fire under it. Then you call on the name of your gods, and I will call on the name of the Lord; and the God who answers by fire, He is God.' So all the people answered and said, 'It is well spoken' " (vv. 22-24).

Elijah proposed bringing the matter to a test, and then he set the rules of engagement:

Select an Animal. Elijah allowed the priests of Baal to choose one of the two available bulls. He would use the other.

Prepare a Sacrifice. The priests would ceremonially prepare the animal and place it on the altar. But they were not to put fire under it. This was the key. Fire was needed for a burnt offering, but this was the test. It had already been proven that Elijah's God controlled the rain (1 Kings 17:1)—now the priests would see that He could also rain fire.

Any of the people of Israel who could have recalled the stories of Moses and Aaron would have known that God had already demonstrated that He could ignite a sacrifice. In Leviticus 9:24, after Moses and Aaron had prepared a sacrifice for the people, this happened: "fire came out from before the Lord and consumed the burnt offering and the fat on the altar. When all the people saw it, they shouted and fell on their faces."

Pray. Elijah told the priests to call on Baal, and he would call on the Lord. The God who answered by fire would be the God who would be worshiped by all. Elijah seemed to give them the advantage by making this a test of fire, for Baal was the sun-god, the god of fire and weather.

The people responded that it was a reasonable proposal, and the test began.

The Prophets are Humiliated

Again, Elijah shows deference to the Baal worshipers by letting them start the contest.

"So they took the bull which was given them, and they prepared it, and called on the name of Baal from morning even till noon, saying, 'O Baal, hear us!' But there was no voice; no one answered. Then they leaped about the altar which they had made" (v.26).

Their Desperation. The prophets of Baal prepared their sacrifice and called out to their god for fire. Their efforts were divided into two segments:

• "From morning even till noon" (v.26), they pleaded for divine fire. "Then they leaped about the altar." What a scene! Still there was no answer, causing Elijah to mock them (v.27).

• The desperation of the prophets continued. They went so far as to "cut themselves . . . with knives and lances, until the blood gushed out on them" (v.28).

They continued throughout the morning and into the afternoon.

• "When midday was passed . . . until the time of the offering of the evening sacrifice" (v.29), they were dancing about, acting in bizarre ways. Yet nothing happened with the altars.

Since Baal was the sun god, perhaps they hoped that at noon, as the sun was at its zenith, the fire would fall on their sacrifice. But their hope turned to despair, and they began to act like lunatics. The result? "There was no voice; no one answered, no one paid attention" (v.29).

Elijah's Mocking. In the meantime, Elijah began to build his case for the true and living God by mocking the priests' feeble attempts at getting Baal to respond. Notice how he exposed Baal's limitations in verse 27:

• "Cry aloud"—yell and make more noise. He can't hear you.

- "For he is a god"—you worship him, but he isn't listening to you.
- "He is meditating"—he may be so deep in thought that you need to get his attention.
- "He is busy"—he may be occupied with someone else's problem or even "relieving himself" (NLT).
- "He is on a journey"—he may have left his house. Call him and bring him back.
- "He is sleeping and must be awakened"—Baal is too weary to help you.

No voice was heard, and no fire was sent. Baal's prophets had failed the test.

Elijah's Preparations are Made

Now it is Elijah's turn. By giving the prophets of Baal the first chance to get fire from their gods, he has set up a dramatic conclusion to the contest. And to that drama, he adds two additional elements: a connection to the twelve tribes of Israel and additional obstacles that have to be overcome in order for his sacrifice to burn.

In verses 30-35, Elijah took charge:

He Summoned the People (v.30). Elijah wanted the people to see what God was going to do. So they left the prophets of Baal and watched him closely.

He Repaired the Broken Down Altar Of God (vv.30-31). There had previously been an altar to Jehovah on that location, probably built during the time of the judges. Elijah chose twelve stones with which to repair the altar—a number that was significant to the people because it signified the twelve tribes of Israel.

He Dug a Trench Around the Altar (v.32). The ditch was made broad and deep.

He Had the People Drench the Altar With Water (vv.33-35). This was done to prevent any suspicion that there was fire hidden under the altar. The altar was repeatedly soaked with water to put the miracle beyond question. Interestingly, they had endured 3 ½ years of drought—so where did they get the water? The only reasonable answer is that they hauled it all the way up from the Mediterranean Sea—at the far western base of the Carmel range! Imagine hauling barrel after barrel of water up that mountain only to dump it on the altar.

So with all the preparations made, Elijah began to pray.

Elijah's Prayer is Given

Elijah's prayer in verses 36-37 was brief. It included statements of:

Identification: "Lord God of Abraham, Isaac, and Israel" (v.36). The Lord was still their God, even though they had left Him and gone after idols.

Vindication: "Let it be known this day that You are God in Israel and I am Your servant, and that I have done all these things at Your word" (v.36). His actions were for God's glory, not Elijah's validation.

Explanation: "Hear me, O Lord, hear me" (v.37). The repetition expresses the burden in his soul.

Notice that Elijah didn't say, "Send fire." This was truly a prayer of faith. He was trusting God for the outcome so completely that the actual request went unspoken. He didn't ask for fire, but he did ask for God to be honored.

God's Power is Displayed

Fire Fell: "Then the fire of the Lord fell and consumed the burnt sacrifice, and the wood and the stones and the dust, and it licked up the water that was in the trench" (v. 38). The fire didn't come from the altar. It fell down from heaven, consuming the sacrifice, wood, stones, water, dust—all of it.

People Fell: "Now when all the people saw it, they fell on their faces; and they said, 'The Lord, He is God! The Lord, He is God!' " (v. 39). The people "fell on their faces" at the sight of God's power (just as had happened in Leviticus 9:24) and acknowledged that Jehovah alone is the God of Israel—not Baal. In reverence for God and in astonishment at the heavenly fire, they turned from their idols and worshiped their God. They had been silent before when Elijah asked them to choose; now they made their choice known.

Prophets Of Baal Fell: "And Elijah said to them, 'Seize the prophets of Baal! Do not let one of them escape!' So they seized them; and Elijah brought them down to the Brook Kishon and executed them there" (v.40).

Elijah Fell: "Then Elijah said to Ahab, 'Go up, eat and drink; for there is the sound of abundance of rain.' So Ahab went up to eat and drink. And Elijah went up to the top of Carmel; then he bowed down on the ground, and put his face between his knees, and said to his servant, 'Go up now, look toward the sea" (vv.41-43). After meeting privately with the king and delivering the message that rain was on the way, Elijah fell before God in prayer. As he prayed, a servant went looking for the answer to the prayer. It came soon enough when he saw clouds forming in the distance (v.44).

Rain Fell: "Now it happened in the meantime that the sky became black with clouds and wind, and there was a heavy rain" (v.45). God's chastening had done its work, and the people had returned to the Lord. The drought was over.

Applying It

What lessons can we draw from this amazing event?

• Matters of truth are not settled by majority vote but by God's Word.

• Sincere and even passionate commitment to the wrong things can be self-destructive.

• Matters of truth and error need powerful, and often uncomfortable, moments of confrontation.

• Discovering the truth about God requires us to make decisions about our faith and the gods of our own culture.

TIMES
OF FRAILTY

FEW EMOTIONS so quickly expose the frailty of men and women as the emotion of despair. When we are battling with our own hearts—regardless of the reason for the struggle—we can find ourselves in a life-and-death war. Despair, that darkest of human emotions, can woo us, entice us, and even destroy us. Sometimes we meet it . . .

- at our job, when we don't get what we think we have earned;

- in our family, when our expectations remain unfulfilled;

- in our church, when we are inevitably disappointed with frail, flawed people;

- in our society, when it seems that the tide is

going the wrong direction.

The battle of the heart is one of the toughest battles a person ever faces, and Elijah would fight this battle in a cave (1 Kings 19:1-18). Remember, Elijah was a man like us—and nowhere is this more obvious than now, as he is caught in the clutches of despair. Here, he becomes a man we can relate to because Elijah's greatest battle was fought, not on Mount Carmel but in a cave at Horeb—not so unlike situations we have all been in. This battle now was not against Baal but against himself.

The Roots of Despair

Ahab told Queen Jezebel what happened on the high place of Carmel: The prophets of Baal (which she had brought to Israel) were dead, and Baal had been overthrown. Her answer? Jezebel sent a message to Elijah: "So let the gods do to me, and more also, if I do not make your life as the life of one of them by tomorrow about this time" (v.2).

In other words, "You will receive the same treatment you gave my prophets—execution."

What was Elijah's response to Jezebel's threat? He fled. Amazingly, the same Elijah who only days before had defeated the prophets of Baal now ran from this woman. The one who had said, "If the Lord is God, follow Him," was now fleeing in despair. What contributed to his despair?

Success. There's often a letdown following moments of great success. In the afterglow of victory, it can be difficult to face the challenges of normal life.

Fatigue. Fatigue often follows intense periods of stress, especially when accompanied by physical exhaustion. This is the "post-Carmel" Elijah—spent, fatigued, and, as a result, vulnerable.

Fear. Jezebel was certainly a woman who could strike fear into the hearts of those who crossed her. And Elijah had done that when he defeated the god she had brought with her from Phoenicia.

When we face a person or a circumstance that seems to be against us and could harm us, it is natural to be fearful. We know Elijah was fearful, for he "ran for his life" (v.2).

Disappointment. It's likely that Elijah was disappointed with the people. On Carmel, they shouted, "The Lord, He is God!" Now they would probably allow him to be killed. At times, despair happens when people don't behave as we think they should.

Loneliness. This is the burden of leadership. In his book *Elijah: A Man Of Like Nature*, Theodore Epp wrote:

> A leader is a lonely man. . . . Driven on by a burning desire to achieve goals that to others seem visionary or impractical, they are looked upon with suspicion by the run-of-the-mill crowd. Men who lead are certain targets for the biting barbs of criticism (p.119).

Elijah had faced much loneliness over the past 42 months. Twice he had faced Ahab alone. He had lived in the wilderness alone for a long period of time. He traveled to and from Zarephath, it seems, by himself. And even as he stood up to all those prophets of Baal, he stood alone. This leader was clearly a lonely man.

These are the roots of Elijah's despair. Weary, just off the mountaintop, fearful, disappointed, and by himself. Elijah had waited 3 ½ years for one glorious day of triumph—and now he was burned out and alone. How did this "man like us" respond to the despair that was creeping into his heart?

The Responses of Despair

Look at the downward steps he followed—steps that would only deepen his sense of despair. His path was understandable but totally wrong.

Desire for Escape. "And when he saw that [the threat from Jezebel], he arose and ran for his life, and went to Beersheba, which belongs to Judah" (v.3). Elijah fled 100 miles to the southern desert. But the grass wasn't any greener there.

Every day, countless people try to escape the difficulties of life—with alcohol, drugs, pleasure. Yet no one escapes problems by running from them. We are our biggest problem.

Desire for Solitude. "[Elijah] left his servant there" (v.3). Loneliness breeds loneliness. Wanting greater solitude, Elijah left his servant and went on alone. Sometimes people who need companionship and friends during tough times push them away in an effort to be by themselves.

Desire for Death. "And he prayed that he might die, and said, 'It is enough! Now, Lord, take my life'" (v. 4). Think of it. Here was the great prophet of God, a man who was just like us but who had stood his ground in some amazing battles, yet now he was ready to check out of this life and its struggles. Sometimes, under stress, death looks like the only way out. Notice that this is Elijah's fifth recorded prayer. He prayed, and . . .

- rain stopped,
- a son returned to life,
- fire fell from heaven, and
- rain returned after 3 ½ years of drought.

All of the first four prayers were answered, but not the fifth. This last one was self-centered. Elijah had lost sight of the power of God. This caused his heart to view death as better than a life of trusting God.

Desert of Self-Pity. "For I am no better than my fathers!" (v. 4). Do you hear him, this man like us? Few things are more tragic than someone filled with self-pity. Elijah felt:

- Everyone else is at fault.
- I am the victim.
- Life is unfair to me.
- I never get ahead.
- I never get a break.

It's easier for us to identify with Elijah here

in the wilderness than on Mount Carmel. Here under a broom tree (v.4) he was more "normal." But God wouldn't leave him there.

The Remedy for Despair

Notice how God dealt with Elijah. He used a blend of tough confrontation and tender compassion to nourish him back to where He wanted him to be. Just as Elijah had to be in training before his great displays of trust and obedience, he again needed God to teach him lessons of divine providence.

Comfort and Care. "So he arose, and ate and drank; and he went in the strength of that food forty days and forty nights as far as Horeb, the mountain of God" (v.8).

God provided Elijah with food and rest to care for his fatigue. Elijah asked for death, but instead God brought him a meal to keep him alive. Sometimes, what we need more than anything else when we're in despair is rest and refreshment.

Without that, we don't have the strength needed to recover. So, in renewed strength, Elijah traveled for 40 more days, stopping at a cave at Horeb.

Confrontation With God in Two Stages

A Powerful Question. "The word of the Lord came to him, and He said to him, 'What are you doing here, Elijah?' " (v.9).

This is a key question. God had sent Elijah to Samaria, Cherith, Zarephath, and Carmel. But He hadn't sent him to Horeb. "Why are you here?" A superficial answer could have been, "I fear Jezebel." But the real answer is seen in Elijah's words of verse 10: "I have been very zealous for the Lord God of hosts; for the children of Israel have forsaken Your covenant, torn down Your altars, and killed Your prophets with the sword. I alone am left; and they seek to take my life."

In other words, "I'm here because I'm unappreciated and full of self-pity." This is a far

99

cry from his bold proclamation on Carmel.

A *Surprising Encounter.* "Then He said, 'Go out, and stand on the mountain before the Lord.' And behold, the Lord passed by, and a great and strong wind tore into the mountains and broke the rocks in pieces before the Lord, but the Lord was not in the wind; and after the wind an earthquake, but the Lord was not in the earthquake; and after the earthquake a fire, but the Lord was not in the fire; and after the fire a still small voice" (vv. 11-12).

God sent messengers from nature—fire, wind, and an earthquake—to remind Elijah that God is God, and that Elijah is not to be ruled by despair. The still small voice of God spoke, and that's when Elijah hid his face (v. 13). He expected the power of God, but he was met by the Person of God. In this place of quiet communion, Elijah was . . .

- reminded of God's power,
- reminded of God's character, and
- reminded of God's love, mercy, and peace.

Call To Help. In verses 15-17, God told Elijah to get involved in the needs of others. He was told to return to the northern kingdom. When he arrived, he was to become involved again in the life of Israel. He was to anoint two kings (Hazael in Syria and Jehu in Israel) and he was to train his own replacement—Elisha.

One key to getting perspective on our despair is to get involved in other people's lives and become concerned for them. An 18th-century writer, John Simpson, put it this way:

> The only hope for persons in such circumstances is to come out from their lonely haunts, and to be actively employed in some useful and benevolent occupations. . . . to set about doing something which will require muscular exertion, and which will benefit others. Hence, God directed Elijah to quit his present lonely abode, which only

increased the sadness and irritation of his spirit; and so He gave him a commission to execute (cited by W. J. Petersen in *Meet Me On The Mountain*, p.120).

The challenge is to get our eyes off ourselves, for only then can we clearly see the needs of others. It's been said, "I cried because I had no shoes; then I met a man who had no feet."

Clarity of Truth. "Yet I have reserved seven thousand in Israel, all whose knees have not bowed to Baal, and every mouth that has not kissed him" (v.18).

Elijah needed a dose of reality to help blast him out of his despair. Our point of view is rarely accurate when seen through despairing eyes. Elijah needed to wake up and see things as they were— not as he had painted them to be. He was not the only faithful servant of God after all (although in 1 Kings 19:10, he had said, "I alone am left").

He was just the only one hiding at Horeb.

Just like Elijah, we love the big wins and the stirring victories. But what about the silent battles of the soul? Elijah thought he was strong, but he had to learn how weak he was and how desperately he needed God. We need to learn that too.

Applying It

God graciously rebuilt Elijah's life out of the ashes of despair and would use him once more. What lessons are here for us?

- Being dedicated to Christ doesn't immunize us from discouragement or despair.

- Fatigue can make us more susceptible to despair.

- We need to invest our energies in others, instead of being absorbed in our pain.

- Communion with God is the only way to maintain the spiritual strength necessary for the battles of life. Rest in His gracious care.

A Final Word

"THE TIME
IT IS TODAY"

THE MUSICAL GROUP The Association sang "The Time It Is Today" in the 1960s, calling young people to live for something more than themselves—to make a difference in the world in their own generation. A similar call comes to followers of Christ today. We are given this moment in time to represent our God in the world. And, like Elijah, we live in extraordinary times.

We can take comfort in the fact that when a great man was expected to ride to the rescue,

God chose an average man—Elijah. This ordinary man, armed only with the resource of praying to an extraordinary God, was God's instrument to have a great impact on an entire generation.

We have seen that Elijah was far from perfect, however. He struggled with the same things we face. That encourages me. If God used a nobody from nowhere like Elijah, perhaps He will use people like us. The challenge, however, is not to pursue greatness but to make ourselves available to our great God's desire to work in us and through us.

If you don't know the God who loves and cares deeply for every person on earth, I have good news: His love has already been fully extended to you. We read in John 3:16, one of the best-known verses in the Bible:

> For God so loved the world that He gave His only begotten Son, that whoever believes in Him should not perish but have everlasting life.

The promise of eternal life is offered to ordinary people by this extraordinary God. Will you accept His free gift? The time—it is today.

NOTES

FOR PERSONAL REFLECTION

NOTES

NOTES